The
Indonesian
Dilemma

THE
INDONESIAN
DILEMMA

Mochtar Lubis

Translated into English by Florence Lamoureux
Published by Graham Brash (Pte) Ltd, Singapore

1977, originally published in Indonesia as *Manusia Indonesia*
     by Idayu Press, Jakarta

1979, translated into English by Florence Lamoureux and
     published as *We Indonesians*
     by Southeast Asian Studies, Asian Studies Program
     University of Hawaii

1983 revised English Edition
     published as *The Indonesian Dilemma*
     by Graham Brash (Pte) Ltd
     36-C Prinsep St
     Singapore 0718

Cover photograph of rice fields in Indonesia by John Lim.

Introduction

On the 6th of April, 1977 Mochtar Lubis electrified a vast audience at the Ismail Marzu Art Centre, Jakarta with his eighty-one page, three-hour lecture entitled, *Situasi Manusia Indonesia Kini: Dilihat dari Segi Kebudayaan dan Nilai Manusia (Indonesians of Today: A Moral and Cultural Evaluation)*. Six days later the lecture was summarised by Alfons Taryadi in *Kompas*, one of the most widely read newspapers in the country. The entire lecture was published (and became a bestseller) in the same year by Idayu Press, Jakarta, under the title, *Manusia Indonesia: Sebuah Pertanggungan Jawab (We Indonesians: Our Responsibility)*.

Mochtar Lubis' speech sparked off reactions all over the country. Among others, Muhan from Pontianak, Jeihan from Bandung and Oom Fan from Jakarta wrote brief, favourable newspaper comments and called on those in power to right what wrongs they could (*Kompas*, 16 April). Further and longer letters and articles by some of the pioneers of the 1945 generation as well as younger intellectuals also appeared in *Kompas* and other leading newspapers such as *Harian Angkatan Bersenjata* and *Sinar Harapan*.

Taking issue with Lubis and indicating his displeasure with what he felt was Lubis' racial slur against the Javanese, Margono Djojohadikusumo, contemporary of the late President Soekarno, stated that what Lubis considered weak traits are in fact part of a well established tradition (particularly among the Javanese) of not hurting or offending others (*Kompas* and *Harian Angkatan Bersenjata*, 13 May).

Kasiyanto attributed the fatalistic attitude of the Javanese, who are quick to accept the unacceptable as God's will, to the natural environment and the effect of Dutch colonialism (*Kompas*, 27 April). Sarlito Wirawan Sarwono (*Kompas*, 5 May) and Ayip Bakar (*Harian Angkatan Bersenjata*, 3 May), while praising Lubis' courage in speaking his mind, questioned the validity of the data from which Lubis drew his conclusions. These articles compelled Lubis to clarify and reassert his position (*Kompas*, 14 May, 1 and 6 June).

Essentially, what Lubis presented is a set of generalisations regarding the Indonesians of today based on his observations of the people around him, not on data or statistics. Although he did not say it, I suspect that these observations were made primarily of civil servants, the military, intellectuals and perhaps also students. After all, these are the people who play the most active political and/or administrative roles in Indonesian society.

In a country where political unity, economic stability and cultural integrity are being sought or reaffirmed, there is a tendency for people to develop an excessive feeling of nationalism which often leads them to think that any view which does not reaffirm the ego, be it that of an individual, an ethnic group, or a nation, is a negative view. On the surface Lubis did speak more of the negatives than the positives. Underneath what he said, however, lie his true motivation and intent. As a keen and frank journalist-observer he speaks in a tone which may sometimes offend, but if we are willing to reflect on what he says, we should be able to see that his view is based very much on what the Javanese call the feeling of *prihatin*, a deep concern arising out of love and care for others. Unfortunately, many people miss this crucial point.

Manusia Indonesia, is one of Lubis' latest *prihatins*. He is greatly concerned that the Indonesians he used to know are undergoing an unfortunate change and if they do not do something about this soon, they will irrevocably lose their old and treasured values. He makes this clear in his response to Margono (*Kompas*, 1 June) who considers the Indonesian aristocracy part of a benign paternalistic tradition. While agreeing with this view, Lubis points out that the type of aristocrats to which Margono refers has become a vanishing breed in our society.

In brief, it is my belief that deep down, underlying his seemingly unfavourable remarks, lies a heartfelt desire to see Indonesia as a strong and well respected nation. The way to achieve this goal is not necessarily through perpetual praise.

Florence Lamoureux has done an excellent job in translating *Manusia Indonesia*. To avoid excessive footnotes, relevant information is incorporated within square brackets in the running text. Lubis' own parenthetical statements are given in parenthesis.

It is hoped that this translation will be read in the same spirit that inspired Mochtar Lubis: a spirit of love and concern for Indonesia.

Soenjono Dardjowidjojo, Ph. D.
Professor of Indonesian
University of Hawaii
1983

The Indonesian Dilemma

Indonesian an old problem ...

The old image is already fading in the mirror, while the local new image is not yet clear...

Who is the new Indonesian? Does he exist? Where is he? What is he like?

Is he a man of strength and courage, a true knight, stylish and impressive, a mixture of Arjuna and Gatotkaca, a Brahman priest or even a Brahman king?

And what is the new woman? Is she like Sukasrana, twin flowing perfumed hair, eyebrows like a delicate line of honey bees, lips like pomegranate and legs as graceful as flipping plants... as described by the Malays?

(Praise the following illustration held true.) Two snobs once were arguing about the origin of Adam and Eve. One of them insisted... They were Javanese.

You're mad, snorted the other. Adam didn't exist then.

Then they were Jews.

That's impossible. The Jews begin with the Prophet Abraham.

The Indonesian Dilemma

The old image is already fading in the mirror, while the typical new image is not yet clear.

Who is the new Indonesian? Does he exist? Where is he? What is he like?

Is he a man of strength and courage, a true knight, stylish and impressive, a mixture of Arjuna[1] and Gatotkaca[2], a Brahman prince or even a Brahman king?

And what of the new woman? Is she like Srikandi[3], 'with flowing perfumed hair, eyebrows like a delicate line of honey bees, lips like pomegranate and legs as graceful as ripening rice plants,' as described by the Malays?

Or does the following illustration hold true? Two sociologists were arguing about the origin of Adam and Eve. One of them insisted, 'They were Egyptian.'

'You're mad,' scoffed the other. 'Egypt didn't exist then.'

'Then they were Jews.'

'That's impossible. The Jews began with the Prophet Abraham.'

---

1 The handsome and refined hero of *The Mahabharata*.
2 Also a hero of *The Mahabharata* and handsome in a more physical sense.
3 Arjuna's beautiful and vivacious wife.

'Well, they must have been Indonesian.'

'Why?'

'Look at them! Adam and Eve had only an apple and a snake. They didn't even have any clothes, and yet they thought they were in paradise!'

Or is it true, as is the opinion of the Chinese merchants who now range across our land, that Indonesians these days can be depicted as having three fingers like THIS? [Lubis rubbed his fingers together — the universal sign of the finger-itch for money.] True or false, I offer this opinion for the audience's consideration. I question the validity of this assessment, but at the same time I hesitate to contradict it because of the following experience:

There were two foreigners, Caucasians, seated in front of me on a plane. Soon after we left Jakarta they became involved in a heated discussion. One of the men said that he was leaving Indonesia for a while because he was bored with just sitting idly in his hotel room. He had waited a long time for all sorts of licences and approvals in order to invest his capital.

'How long have you been waiting?' asked his friend.

'Hell, four months already, coming up to five.'

'You're going about it the wrong way. Don't you know that in Jakarta money speeds up everything? You know what I mean ..... You can buy anybody in Jakarta.'

Blood rose to my head. I am a citizen of Jakarta and that was an extraordinary insult. I wanted to strike the rude lout across the mouth, but common sense told me that if I hit him, I might be whisked off to court where I would probably have lost the case. So I just calmed down. Whether or not such foreigners are justified in their opinion of us in Jakarta, I leave you to decide. Is there anyone here who would have dared to take issue with these foreigners in a court of law and prove their allegations untrue?

What of the past and present opinions of others concerning Indonesians? When they first reached our shores the Dutch considered us dishonest, dishonourable, treacherous, belligerent, brutal and no better than animals. On the other hand, the Indonesians accused the Dutch of not honouring their promises and of perpetrating such cruelty that they were merely being repaid in kind. Even after the Dutch had colonised the country and had come to know the Indonesians better, the general opinion remained that the 'natives' lacked the intelligence and integrity to take on responsible jobs and were a mediocre lot, barely acquainted with religion, hard work, honesty, sympathy, gratitude and the finer human instincts.

Not until much later did the Dutch credit the Indonesian people with possessing any good qualities. Even then it was still thought that Indonesians lacked a mind of their own, were weak-willed, indecisive and easily led. It was said of the various ethnic groups that the Irianese were rowdy and quick to anger; the Macassarese and Buginese were persevering — able to endure fatigue and suffering; the Balinese had a zest for life and were hard-working, but also brutal; the Ambonese were intelligent and independent; the Malays were suspicious and aloof but could sometimes be most hospitable; the Bataks, Acehnese, Mandailings and Menangs were hard-headed; the Javanese were conceited and over-sensitive and they made good yes-men.

3

In 1416 a Chinese Moslem named Ma Huan, the interpreter to Cheng Ho, travelled to our archipelago and visited Java. He wrote that there were three types of people here:

1) the Moslems who came from areas west of Indonesia and who now lived here. Their food and clothing were clean and good.

2) the Chinese living in Indonesia, many of whom had embraced Islam and faithfully followed the teachings of the Prophet. Their food and clothing were excellent.

3) the indigenous people who were disgustingly dirty and shabby. They went about with uncombed hair and bare feet and lived in fear of all kinds of evil spirits. They ate half raw snakes, ants, bugs, worms and other repulsive things. They ate the meat of dogs and they also slept with them .....

First Characteristic

What can we say about those Indonesians who claim to be religious? According to the Islamic leaders on television and lecturers on religion, the Indonesian Moslem is devout, pious, faithful in attending religious services, honest and true to the teachings of Mohammed, s.a.w.[1], who said that a Moslem is one who has the courage to tell the truth even to a cruel despot and who considers malicious jealousy and religious betrayal taboo. God's laws must always be obeyed, and His followers must always be fully prepared to oppose evil. When a Moslem sees an evil situation and has neither the power nor the courage to change it, then he must verbally admonish the person responsible for it. If that too accomplishes nothing, the Moslem will at least have reinforced his own faith.

---

1 An abbreviation of the Arabic *salla'llahu'alihi'wassallama*, which translates: May the Lord bless him (Mohammad) and give him peace.

4

Christians and followers of other religions should also be like that. The ideal Indonesian of any faith adheres to the teachings of his religion, shows equal love for all people and, in fact, complies with the Ten Commandments of Christianity.

How many Indonesians, whatever their religion, really live according to the teachings of their faith? I refer not just to weekly church attendance, going to confession, devoutly attending the mosque or fasting, but to practising one's religion in one's daily behaviour. Again, I leave the answer to you.

I perceive a chasm developing between our ideal Indonesian and our actual Indonesian, the latter meaning all of us here. A great gap exists between our pretences and our realities.

Let us take a look at what is going on around us. One legacy of the animistic era of our great-grandfathers is the strong presence of myths and mystiques in our society today. We have always taken great pleasure in creating myths and do so with relative ease. The old ones are cherished and we make up new ones as well to give us courage and confidence to face crises and various difficulties when we are unable to tackle them with the power of rational thought. Our superstitious beliefs, old and new, are used as a shield to ward off approaching threats and dangers.

Mysticism, which is popularly referred to as *kebatinan* [the inner self], is a constant refuge of those in doubt or difficulty. This is true of almost everyone, whether he be religious or a professedly rational thinker. Even those who have the highest education are not immune. Among highly rational and well educated Indonesians — skilled mathematicians, nuclear physicists who can separate the smallest atom — there are

5

many who are attracted to *kebatinan*. Their motives are varied: a need for reassurance or a hunger for power, position or wealth. Because this mystical ideology has control of the largest segment of Indonesia's population, especially those on the island of Java, it is probably a good idea to take a moment to examine the Javanese mystics so that we can understand our people better.

According to the initiated the main objective of *kebatinan* is to achieve unity — a unity which will encompass all. Furthermore, *kebatinan* views human beings as consisting of two elements, the inner and the outer. Both of these are God-given. The believer considers the inner life to be his real life. The outer man is only the body with all its wants, needs and weaknesses. The mystic calls it *jagad cilik* [materialistic world] and believes the human spirit must dominate it. A man who is in control of his *jagad cilik* has reached the ultimate level and is king/hero/priest all in one. He is in command of both his mind and his body and has achieved unity with the spiritualism which God ordained. Thereafter his body undergoes a spiritual process and he reaches a spiritual and physical accord. He is at peace with himself and other men. He is in tune with nature and God. Buddha called this attaining *Nirvana*. The ideal *kebatinan* man works diligently without ulterior motives.

Our Javanese brothers are tireless in their pronouncement: *sepi ing pamrih rame ing gawe, amemayu ayuning bawana* [work hard without seeking personal reward, and you will make the world progress], and they spend their lives working as God's messengers in this transitory world. According to Javanese spiritualism the ideal Indonesian must have the following characteristics: resignation to God's will, willingness to give away his possessions where necessary, and patience — indeed, his life is one of patience and tolerance.

I leave it to you to decide whether or not this ideal can be found in our country. For hundreds of years various Javanese spiritual ideologies have existed among. Have they produced such a man?

Finally, the ideal man of today is said to be one who believes in *Pancasila*, the five principles of which are: faith in God, humanitarianism, social justice, democracy and national unity. The *'Pancasilaist'* is an exemplary man who possesses all the human ideals derived from religious teachings and mythical ideologies as well ideals derived from various political creeds. Have we seen a *Pancasila* man among us? Again, I leave the answer to you.

Besides all the many religions, philosophies and mysticisms that have confronted Indonesians, we have also been bombarded with modern science and technology, a variety of political ideologies such as democracy, socialism, communism, etc., and all sorts of value systems from all corners of the world. We have been ravished by the Portuguese, the Spanish, the Dutch, the Japanese, the Chinese and other peoples, and for the last thirty years by international consumerism and greed-orientated multi-national enterprises, not to mention our own selfish people.

We are also known for our syncretic powers. We retain the old and accept the new and they exist together within us in incongruous harmony. As good Moslems we pray five times a day, but we also make sacrifices to Dewi Sri [Goddess of Prosperity] or put flowers under a sacred banyan tree. As good Christians we go to church, and then we go on to a pagan shrine to be blessed. One foot is still planted in our animistic culture while the other is in the modern age with all its rapidly changing values, where we always seem to be at least twenty years behind. Between our two feet are alter-

7

nating layers of ancient and modern influences. It seems to me that one of our weaknesses is that we lack the ability to choose between these influences so that they co-exist indiscriminately within us. Our faith as Moslems or Christians exists side by side with our belief in the powers of the sacred tree or Dewi Sri. Religious people do not feel embarrassed or irresponsible when they go to a faith healer or look for prophetic omens in the stars, glasses of water, dreams or other sources of prophecy.

For example, I was shocked to read that well educated men like Sawito and Sujono[1] still look to the mountains, the forests and caves for *wahyu* [messages from God], and that their decisions and actions are based on such *wahyu*. Imagine what would happen if our government policies were dependent on *wahyu* and irrational guidance. What a dangerous way to govern our lives!

What if my imprisonment during Soekarno's regime had been based on the following incident: one night either Soekarno or his *dukun* [adviser in mysticism] had a dream that the president was climbing a high mountain when he slipped and fell. The next morning the *dukun* advised Soekarno to beware of tall men. [Lubis is exceptionally tall.]

Views on the nature of man are many and varied. Islam considers each baby to be *tabula rasa* — untouched and holy. Christianity, on the other hand, teaches that man is born sinful and can redeem his soul only through prayer and repentance. Protestants and Calvinists go even further and

---

1 In 1976 these men claimed to have received a message from God telling them that Indonesia's leadership should be replaced. So fervent was their belief that one of them, Sawito, drew up a petition to this effect which was signed by several influential men including the former vice president, Mohammad Hatta. This created a political incident which resulted in Sawito being jailed.

believe that hard work should be part of man's service to God. This work ethic is prevalent in European and American businesses. Some of those who advocate the *Pancasila* way of life seem to think that *Pancasila* values are exclusively Indonesian and will solve all our problems. I earnestly hope and pray that we will succeed in achieving the ideals of *Pancasila* by the year 2000. When this happens, Indonesia will surely be heaven on earth and each of us will lead a life of joy and bliss. But we are not there yet. On the contrary, we still have miles to go. In the meantime we must continue to try and live in harmony, all of us here in this auditorium and all those millions of people outside this building.

What are we really like today? Do we have the appearance of little monkeys or of Arjuna? Are we like Kalongwewe[1] or Princess Sinta[2]? Suppose that I were a great *dukun* with the power to conjure up a magic mirror. If it were placed before the Indonesian people of today, what would they see? I ask you, with your keen eyesight, to join me in looking into this mirror. I hope you will correct me if I see less or more than is actually there.

In general we can say that our physical appearance is not displeasing. Many foreigners consider us a handsome race. They praise our attractive features and slender bodies; our men with lithe, well muscled frames, cheerful faces, ebony hair and bronze complexions; our lovely women with refined voices, graceful movements and other fine attributes. Indonesian men are handsome enough. We can observe the success of the homosexuals in Jakarta selling their prime commodity. If you want to discuss Indonesian women, I would gladly say

1 A repugnant ghost with long, shaggy hair and pendulous breasts.
2 Wife of Rama in *The Ramayana* and a representative of the best qualities of womanhood.

more about them. The magic mirror reflects no distortion whatsoever there. They are among the most beautiful women in the world.

But I digress. Let us now use this mirror to examine our inner selves. Will we also see beautiful things there? Yes, we do indeed see some beauty within us. The sensitivity of our artists is acute. They live in harmony with nature and are inspired by their environment. For them the mountains, forests, rivers, sea, sky, stars and moon are full of mystery and beauty which seem to escape our ordinary senses.

In past ages our artistic talent and love of beauty inspired tremendous creative expression throughout the archipelago. Witness our temples, sculptures, wood carvings, weaving, gold and silver work, written and oral literature, music and dance. Foreign influences have diminished our present artistic accomplishments, but I feel sure that the talent lies latent within us and can emerge again, given the proper artistic climate. Our imaginative and creative abilities are inferior to none.

Something happened, however, in the historical development of the Indonesian people. From the *Jahiliah* era [the turbulent pre-Islamic period], when our forefathers still lived in a primitve fashion, Indonesians such as Bataks and Lampungs already had written languages. Several social systems existed then, too. Their values might now be considered unsuitable: for example, the old Batak practice of eating their enemies who were killed in battle or condemned to death. Consider also the Dayak and West Irian head-hunters. Scholars who have conducted detailed studies of the Batak head-hunters have concluded that the Batak social system cannot be understood unless we fully comprehend the nature of cannibalism at that time. A person who was killed in a war

10

or who was executed because he had broken the law had to be consumed by the entire group in order to legalise the killing or the death sentence. In this way strength or supernatural power was derived from the sacrificial victim.

We may not uphold those ancient values. We would like to see, for example, the complete abolition from our country of the tyranny and slavery which were part of our past. Nevertheless, labelling those times as totally *Jahiliah* is not completely accurate. For instance, during the same period, even before the advent of Hinduism, the Javanese had already developed a fairly sophisticated social system. There were villages which were in effect self-governing, small social units which were ruled democratically. Witness the village system in Minangkabau and the government in Mandailing where the king was regarded as the father of his subjects. Of course, some charlatans could always be found among those rulers.

We should take note of the broadening of Indonesian artistic development during those ancient times. Creativity was given further impetus with the introduction of Hinduism on Sumatra, Java and Bali. The influence of Islam and Christianity came later and drastically curbed that artistic creativity — especially with regard to sculpture which had flourished under the ancient Indonesian religions. For example, when the Paderis attacked the Tapanulis in Sumatra, bringing Islam at the point of the sword, they destroyed some of the finest sculpture in Indonesia and forbade the creation of any new works. Later on this same policy was continued by the Christian church in Batak and Karo on the island of Nias and several eastern Indonesian islands. With the spread of Islam on Java, sectors of the population moved to Bali, taking their old religion and their artistic talents with them. In West Irian also the Christian church opposed the creation of new sculptures, but several of the American missionaries there, who were also talented traders, did not burn or destroy the existing sculptures. Instead they sent them off to be sold in the United States.

The Indonesian's attitude toward sex underwent a tremendous change with the advent of Islam and then Christianity. To the peoples of Polynesia and Indonesia sex had been a very natural thing. This attitude is still prevalent in the sexual activities of various West Irian tribes which have not yet fully accepted Islam or Christianity. It can also be found in the customs and daily relationships between young men and women in Mandailing and Batak areas which have been labelled flirtatious [*mermaiyam*]. In some of these tribes premarital relationships are quite common.

The power of sexual attraction to Indonesians is reflected in the following poems:

Melayu:

Air dalam bertambah dalam	Deep waters grow deeper,
Hujan dahulu belum lagi teduh	Yesterday's rain has not ceased.
Hati dendam bertambah dendam	My heart yearns more fiercely,
Dendam dahulu belum lagi sembuh.	Yesterday's longings unappeased.
Berbentung guruh di papan	Thunder resounds from the wood,
Kilatnya sampai ke Selayang	Lightning flashes at Selayang.
Tujuh sorga di dalam badan	Within the body seven paradises,
Itulah makna kasih sayang.	Such is the promise of love.

Sunda:

Kamana hambirung jangkung	Where is the tall *hambirung* tree?
Barang tuwar pilisungeun	Fell it and make a rice pestle.
Kamana nu hideung jangkung	Where is the tall handsome man?
Urang syiar pibatureun.	I want him for my lover.
Ki ranca dijalan ka Kaduguling	*Ki ranca* tree on the road to Kaduguling,
Pancuran awi sabebek	Water pours from the bamboo pipe.
Nyi randa gulang-guling	The widow tosses restlessly in her sleep,
Lakian hayang ka dewek.	Longing me for desperately.
Ngala hunbut ngala jantung	Gather the blossoms and heart of the banana plant,
Ngala ower dikojaan	Gather *ower* at Kojaan.
Hayang imut jeung nu jangkung	I want to enjoy the tall handsome fellow,
Hayang noel ngabogaan.	I want to touch and possess him.

Jawa:

Jula juli sarung pekalongan	The *jula juli* sarong from Pekalongan
Seringgit selikur etje	Costs two and a half rupiahs.
Dak perduli gendak colongan	Who cares if she's false-hearted?
Tak anggit bojoku dewe.	I will make her mine.

13

Melayu:

Imbang-imbang di pintu
kembang
Sayur bayam saya tumiskan
Bimbang siang boleh
ditahan
Bimbang malam jadi
tangisan.

Flowers bloom at the door,

I stir-fry some spinach.
Longing can be restrained
by day,
At night it becomes
unbearable.

Mandailing:

Muda mandurung ko di
pahu
Tampul si mardulang-dulang
Muda malungun ko di au
Tetep si tumondang bulan.

When they climb upon the
fern tree,
Cut down the caladiums.
When you yearn for me,
Gaze at the full moon.

Melayu:

Dimana kuang bertelur

Di atas lata di ruang batu

Di mana abang nak tidur
Di atas dada di ruang susu.

Where lays the forest hen
her egg?
In the roots among the
rocks.
Where do I wish to sleep?
In the hollow between your
breasts.

Minangkabau:

Sirambah anak dari pakan

Didabieh lalu dipanggang-
kan

Sirambah is brought from
the market,
Slaughtered and barbecued.

Hamba tidak lengah di adik	You, my love, I can never forget,
Siang menjadi angan-angan	By day you are my fantasy,
Malam hari masuk rasian.	At night my tortured dream.

As an example of sexual permissiveness in former times, here is another verse:

Ke Teluk sudah, ke Siam sudah	I've been to Teluk, I've been to Siam,
Ke Mekah saja saya yang belum	I've not yet been to Mecca.
Berpeluk sudah bercium sudah	I've been hugged, I've been kissed,
Bernikah saja saya yang belum.	I've never yet been married.

Folk tales like the story of Kabayan[1] in West Java clearly show the Indonesian's sexuality and sensuality. The Javanese 'drug store' provides a variety of aphrodisiacs and sex manuals. South Sulawesi has come up with some unique sexual paraphernalia, and the men of Kalimantan boast of their *pasak bumi* [a potion to increase male sexual prowess]. In olden times in some of our tribes men pierced their sexual organs with star-like devices, much as women do their ears, to enhance their partners' sexual pleasure.

We all realise that sexual attraction is a powerful drive and affects every man's behaviour. When he is so pressured, all sorts of psychological and complex situations arise. In this way we can see how the oppressive new influences inhibited the creativity of our people. There have been a lot of pres-

---

1 A cunning folk hero who sometimes displays lecherous characteristics.

sures on and changes in the sexual attitude of the individual Indonesian. (At least it looks that way from the outside.) Over and above this there were also greater and unfamiliar influences such as the waves of Westerners bringing the values and cultures of their own societies.

Our history is that of an oppressed people. The ancient Indonesian kings were despots, convinced that they ruled by divine right. These tyrants could murder at will and such evil was not considered to be a violation of the law. They held the people's lives in their hands. The kings were thought to have supernatural powers, and it was believed that even their belongings and clothes were possessed of these powers so that they could not be used, worn or copied by others. Our people believed that the kings' powers extended even further and that if they desired, they could bring back the dead. They could also return from the grave themselves. In some areas they exercised 'the right of the king' or, as the French would put it, *le droit du siegneur*, to deflower a young virgin who was about to be married.

The ancient Javanese kings enjoyed watching combats, usually between wild animals such as tiger against tiger, or tiger against water buffalo, but sometimes between tiger and condemned prisoner. The combat arenas were surrounded four deep with troops armed with spears to prevent the beast's escape. The officer who opened the starving animal's cage was not allowed to dash to safety once the animal was free. He had to pay homage to the king and then make a slow and polite exit. If the tiger left its enclosure too quickly and attacked the man, then that poor soldier suffered an unfortunate fate. He had, however, been killed in the line of duty and perhaps a posthumous gift, a medal, would eventually be awarded to him. If the tiger attacked the guards surrounding the arena and some of these men were killed, that was of no great significance. They were merely performing their duty: guarding their king who was enjoying the entertainment.

Needless to say, there were many types of labour which the king and nobility extracted from the populace without any renumeration, not to mention the confiscation of the people's water buffaloes and rice, as later reported by Multatuli[1].

Through various levels of influence, oppression and suppression, we have developed into what we now call Indonesians. There were times during our revolution when we felt that we would be able to free our bodies and souls from all forms of restriction and emerge as new men with spirits intact. In reality, very few of us have succeeded in throwing off the shackles of the past centuries.

A prominent Indonesian characteristic is hypocrisy. The man who pretends one thing to a person's face and says another behind his back has been around for a long time, ever since Indonesians were forced to conceal their true feelings for fear of reprisal. Our feudal system was so oppressive that it stifled all initiative among the people and promoted this terrible hypocrisy. In later years several religions were introduced which raised our spiritual standards, but religion has never been a fully liberating force because it came with sword and cannon in league with invaders and colonial masters.

There is hypocrisy in our attitude toward sex. Publicly we condemn overt sexuality. Foreign magazines and publications with pictures of nude or partly nude bodies must have such illustrations deleted before they can be sold in Indonesia.

---

1 Pen name of Eduard Dowes Dekker, author of *Max Havelaar*, a novel exposing conditions in Indonesia under Dutch rule.

This is done so as not to offend the feelings of decent Indonesians. At the same time, however, we have saunas and massage parlours. We regulate prostitution — we protect it. We protect the girls and their customers in a variety of ways: official, semi-official, or private.

Because of such attitudes, Indonesia is ridden with hypocrisy. At home we pretend piety, but the moment an Indonesian gets off the plane in Singapore, Hong Kong, Paris, New York or Amsterdam, he hops into a taxi and looks for a nightclub, or goes to a hotel where he orders a porter or bellboy to find him a girl. He condemns corruption, but he himself is corrupt.

We all speak against corruption or, in the new terminology, *komersialisasi jabatan* [bribery, favouritism], but we continue to act corruptly, and this despicable trait becomes more entrenched all the time. The attitude of such hypocritical Indonesians is just the sort of thing that enabled the intense corruption in Pertamina, the national oil company, to go on for so many years. Although the facts in this case are clear, to this day no legal action has been taken against those important executives who were involved.

We constantly proclaim that our laws apply equally to all people. In practice, however, the petty thief goes to jail while the big-time thief goes free or is jailed for only a very short while.

The consequence of this hypocrisy, which is rooted deeper than our colonial past, is that present-day Indonesians have become masters of the ABS [*Asal Bapak Senang* — 'yes-man'] practice. This ABS attitude may be traced back to feudal times when the lords oppressed the people, who hid behind figurative masks to protect themselves from the

18

excessive demands of these rulers. To protect their property and preserve their lives, people were compelled to be dishonest with themselves and others by always saying, 'Yes, Your Majesty; yes, Your Grace; yes, My Lady; yes, master; yes, boss; yes, sir; etc.'

The hypocritical attitude, which was instilled in Indonesians by other Indonesians who were stronger and who squeezed, robbed and violated our people, was intensified by foreign powers. The Portuguese and Spanish, who were in turn followed by the Dutch, treated large sectors of our people with cruelty and harshness. This drove hypocrisy yet deeper into the Indonesians. They behaved even more hypocritically in order to 'survive' — a term popular today in our country. People have become continually more clever at hiding their real feelings, thoughts and even convictions.

We have learned to say 'no' in so many ways that the actual word 'no' has become quite unfamiliar to us. This holds true with any kind of dissent. Disagreement and criticism are expressed in devious ways. Right up to this moment, and I don't know how long it's going to last, this attitude continues to exist in the hearts of Indonesians. The leaders are eager to be praised and the followers eager to praise.

Our country's struggle for freedom brought the promise of democracy, dignity, piety, equality and justice for all. Yet the whole nation goes along with and takes part in this hypocritical farce. The sultan, whom we once glorified with the title 'Lord', we now address as *bapak* [originally father, now also means a high-ranking or older man]. In truth, this father-child relationship is not a democratic element in our culture. The father is the authority figure and the child must obey. Right? This attitude also encourages intellectual treason in our country.

19

Second Characteristic

The second characteristic predominant among Indonesians today is a tendency for 'buck-passing'. 'I didn't do it,' has become an all too common Indonesian expression. There is an evasion of responsibility for errors and things done inadequately or poorly. Blame is passed on to a subordinate who in turn passes it on to another subordinate and so one downwards a hundredfold. We can count on the fingers of one hand those leaders throughout our history who were brave and moral enough to accept the responsibility for the wrongdoing which occurred under their rule.

In dealing with this attitude of not wanting to accept the blame for the things that go wrong, the subordinate also has an answer. He is always quick to defend himself with, 'I only did what my boss told me to do.' In the final analysis, no one is ever responsible for failure.

We can use Pertamina as a prime example of this irresponsible attitude. Hundreds of millions of dollars of our country's wealth were lost and various laws and regulations were violated by a variety of officials, from the director, Ibnu Sutowo, downwards. Yet, not one person has been prosecuted. According to *The Herald Tribune* of 24 December, 1976 Ibnu Sutowo acknowledged in a court in New York that he had violated Indonesian law when he became a member of the advisory council of the Geneva Intermaritime Bank. This was during the case against a Panama business managed by a Mr. Bruce Rappaport, a business associate of Ibnu Sutowo. Rappaport held shares in that bank (and there is a good chance that Sutowo was also involved there). It was said that Sutowo had signed 1,600 promissory notes without first reading them. He gave them to Bruce Rappaport to soothe nervous business associates. He admitted also that he had asked Rappaport for a loan of two and a half million dollars and then put that money in a private bank account and never repaid the loan. How generous of Mr. Rappaport, if Ibnu's story was true. But we can see here that the money must have been intended for distribution among those involved.

On the other hand, when there is praise to be apportioned, Indonesians are not reluctant to step forward and receive gold stars, applause, letters of commendation, medals, etc. If, however, we examine a list of these gold star or even guerilla star recipients, we can see that the majority of those who were given this 'Great Son' medal, and other similar tokens of appreciation and esteem, were members of the *bapak* class. The small time officials, or those of even lower rank, who work diligently and patiently endure all sorts of difficulties, seldom get the rewards which are due to them.

Third Characteristic

The third main characteristic of Indonesians is a feudal mentality. Although one of the aims of our revolution was to free our people from feudalism, new forms of it are constantly springing up in our society. This feudal attitude can be seen in our official state ceremonies and in the relationships within groups of civil servants. Examine the leadership in women's organisations. In military or civil servant circles, for instance, it is the wives of the top men who are elected to be leaders. The commander's wife and the minister's wife automatically become chairmen, not because of their abilities, leadership talents, knowledge, expertise, or even their devotion to their groups.

The feudal spirit permeates all strata of society. Rank and power depend on wealth or one's level in the military or civil service hierarchy. The vassals serve the lords for a number of reasons and in a number of ways; they show obedience, respect, fear; they humble themselves, are overly polite, know their places and accept them; and they never miss an opportunity to please the *bapak*. In short, they must behave with an ABS mentality to avoid displeasing the *bapak*.

There is nothing more ridiculous than the role of telephones in Indonesian society. Once a friend told me this story. He wanted to telephone a bigwig. A secretary answered his call and he asked to speak with her boss. She replied, 'Do you have an appointment?' He was amazed and said, 'What, do you mean I need an appointment for a phone call!' The problem is that many people feel that a direct telephone call to a person in an important position smacks of discourtesy. Our feudalistic mind dictates that the ease of using a phone indicates a diminishing of respect. The polite way to contact a VIP is to go in person to meet him. The waiting may take from several days to several weeks. The longer one waits, the more prestigious the person who keeps him waiting. A secretary will proudly announce that if you want an appointment with *bapak* so and so it won't be easy. The shortest wait is two weeks. He is busy all the time and works tirelessly.

We say that we want modernisation, we want to implement modern technology, we want to make more use of the Palapa Satellite[1], we want more telephone communications, and yet to place a phone call to an executive or an official in a higher position than oneself is considered disrespectful. Ridiculous, isn't it?

The civil service in Mentawai orders young men to cut their hair short as part of the process of modernising the Mentawai

---

1 Advanced communications satellite purchased by the Indonesian government.

tribe. At the same time the men, young and old, in Jakarta are wearing their hair long. In Fiji students attend school half-naked. That's modernisation. In West Irian the loincloth was frowned on and is no longer worn, but in Jakarta nightclubs strippers are featured attractions.

This feudal mentality has always exerted a pressure on the Indonesian attitude toward authority. In ancient days the king's power was believed to be an extension of God's power. In those times Malay people were forbidden to wear anything yellow because that colour signified the king's power. This sacred quality applied not only to the king, but to his entire family and even to his possessions such as his sword, his kris, his clothes, and his *destar* [Malay or Sumatran head-dress]. It was believed that the Javanese kings had God-given vision, and therefore, they could do no wrong and every word they spoke was the truth. As long as they adhered to these divine revelations their actions and words would always be correct. This belief held true for all Indonesians throughout our archipelago. The kings of ancient Java, Bali, Sumatra, Sulawesi, and the Malay Peninsula all had this type of ruler-subject relationship. It continues right up to today. The king's title has given way to president, minister, general, secretary general, director general, university president, governor, president or director of a large privately owned business, plantation manager, etc. Although their forms have changed, feudal relationships are alive and well in Indonesian society.

Those in power do not like to be criticised, and their subordinates are very reluctant to criticise them. The result is the same as before. The power centre maintains very little communication with the common people. Communication is always from the top downwards and never the other way around. The traffic is strictly one way.

23

A situation like this complicates the development processes of our people since the well being of a society depends heavily on how efficiently or ineptly a country absorbs economic, political, technical knowledge, etc. The outlook for correcting this lord-vassal relationship either from the top down or from the bottom up appears rather bleak. If the person in power finds anything displeasing, he will normally take repressive action. The efforts and processes involved in preventing the development of an undesirable situation, however, seem to be thoroughly understood by each sector, yet it is virtually impossible to change anything in this feudal type of situation. The underling is afraid to suggest new and different ideas which might conflict with those of the 'establishment'. He lacks the courage to criticise a superior. Likewise, he lacks the nerve to present any facts which might displease the *bapak*. The *bapak* is content with the feudal attitude that power is synonymous with wisdom and ingenuity, that he is all-knowing and perfect.

Fourth Characteristic

The fourth main Indonesian characteristic is belief in superstition. Not only in the early days, but now as well, there are those of us who still believe that stones, mountains, beaches, rivers, lakes, coral, trees, statues, buildings, krises, knives, and swords all have mysterious powers. Man must somehow establish a special relationship with these things. In order to please the spirits and prevent their alienation, they must be worshipped and offered sacrifices. Graves must be sprinkled with water and flowers, covered with yellow, red, or white cloth, and someone must read a prayer, bring a tribute or sacrifice, and ask for a blessing.

Indonesians believe in auspicious and inauspicious times. They believe, too, in a variety of natural omens. If a crow circles above a house everyone within is terrified since it is supposed to mean a death will occur in that home. It is taboo to pass under a clothes-line. If it is unavoidable, the person going under the line must throw a stone over it. Tigers are sacred. There are those among us who believe that their fore-fathers were tigers, and if these people are in the forest they dare not utter the word 'tiger'. In Minangkabau the tiger is called 'Granny', because these people are afraid of possible retaliation if the animal is referred to otherwise.

The kris is considered very sacred. It is carefully washed, bathed in incense vapours, and sheathed in silk or velvet. Many people are afraid to hold a kris, let alone to possess one. If the holder's personality and that of the kris are not in harmony, the kris will bring trouble to the holder. There are, however, good luck krises which can guard souls and wealth. There are krises which can make their owners invulnerable and invisible in battle. There are also krises which can fly from one place to another. In addition to krises, there are other weapons and objects which are considered to be sacred, supernaturally powerful, and can protect or betray a person.

Indonesians believe in all sorts of ghosts, monsters, genies, and supernatural beings. We also believe in the sacredness of *gamelans* and gongs which can be played only at certain times.

The belief that man can change his physical appearance into that of an animal, is commonly accepted throughout our country. On Java, the Sundanese believe in *ngepet*, that is, a belief that people change into pigs, dogs, or other animals in order to become rich [for instance, by stealing money from others]. In Sumatra, too, many people firmly believe that human beings have the ability to change their physical appearance at will.

Because of these beliefs Indonesians are expert symbol-makers. Many believe in amulets and magic formulas. We put offerings and flowers in the four corners of our yards to chase away ghosts. To avoid bad luck or disaster we throw seven kinds of flowers into the middle of a crossroad. We compose incantations and recite them, and, along with the amulets, they make us feel that we have done our best to ensure our good health and happiness.

Even now modern, educated Indonesians still make talismans, repeat incantations, and create symbolic slogans. One of our country's most powerful slogan-makers was none other than the late president Soekarno. During the Japanese occupation his chants of *Amerika Kita Seterika* [Flatten America] and *Inggeris Kita Linggis* [Gouge the British] caused many Indonesians to become intoxicated with the idea that we were indeed powerful enough to do these things. Later, under his own rule, his mantras became even greater in influence. e.g.; Nekolim[1], Vivere Pericoloso[2], Berdikari[3], Jarek[4], Usdek[5], Resopim[6], and so on, until we came to a time when we were free of his visions and realised that all of his incantations and amulets were void of meaning.

Later we made new slogans and sayings — new talismans: Tritura[7], Ampera[8], the new order, rule of law, fight against corruption, prosperity and justice for all, and intellectual development. Indonesians are very much inclined to believe in symbols, mottos, and sayings which they themselves create. Our country is based on *Pancasila*. We all say this and then we stop and smugly sit back fully satisfied that, having expressed it, we have therefore created a *Pancasila* society. It is no different from a magician who says abracadabra and pulls a rabbit from a hat. Yet *Pancasila* has still to be reflected in our country's legislation as far as taxes on wealth and inheritance, guarantees for social welfare, guarantees for the sick and the old, and laws requiring equal educational opportunities for rich and poor alike are concerned.

Indonesians are inclined to believe that if these things have already been thought of, discussed, and agreed upon then the result of the plan is already realised. I am convinced that drawers in government offices and private organisations are filled with documents and reports of decisions arrived at in meetings, committees and councils which have never been executed.

We now create superstitions from a variety of things in our modern world. Modernisation is a new superstition, as is economic development. Industrial nations are held up as models and as such are new symbols with all the attending amulets and mantras which are associated with increasing the gross national product or the gross domestic product. Yet all the time we fail to see the damage to our values and our well being. We are blind to the ruining and poisoning of our environment and our natural resources by the progressive economies and technologies of the developed countries.

---

1   Acronym for *Neokolonialisme* — neo-colonialism.

2   To Live Dangerously — from the title of Soekarno's speech of August 17, 1965.

3   Acronym for *Berdiri di atas Kaki Sendiri* — Standing on one's own feet, from Soekarno's August 17, 1965 speech.

4   Acronym for *Jalannya Revolusi Kita* — The March of Our Revolution.

5   Acronym for *Undang-Undang Dasar 1945, Socialisme Indonesia, Demokrasi Terpimpin, Ekonomi Terpimpin, Kepribadian Indonesia* — The 1945 Constitution, Indonesian Socialism, Guided Democracy, Guided Economy, Indonesian Identity.

6   Acronym for *Revolusi, Socialisme (Indonesia), Pimpinan Nasional* — Revolution, (Indonesian) Socialism, National Leadership. Title of Soekarno's 1961 Independence Day address.

7   Acronym for *Tri Tuntutan Rakyat* — The Three Demands of the People. These demands which were made in 1966 were: 1) Demand to ban the Communist Party, 2) Demand to reconstitute the cabinet, and 3) Demand to lower prices.

8   Acronym for *Amanat Penderitaan Rakya*, Message of the People's Suffering. Title of a speech Soekarno delivered to the cabinet in July 1966.

Technology, modernisation, planning, industrialisation, production, modern science and multi-national corporations are our new mantras and symbols today. We say little about just and equal distribution of wealth and fail to examine closely the negative side of all that we wish to imitate and bring into our society.

If we say the word 'modernisation', a picture usually comes into our minds. We visualise large factories with tall chimneys which belch thick, black smoke into the atmosphere, cars and trucks zig-zagging on infinite freeways and giant cities filled with skyscrapers. Who wouldn't like to brag about the Wisma Nusantara as the tallest building in Southeast Asia? In our mind's eye we see TV sets, electronic devices and a variety of small appliances for home and office. We also visualise every Indonesian owning a car, a motorcycle, an air-conditioned house and so on. We imagine these things because we are exposed to international consumerism through advertising in newspapers, TV, movies and billboards. Take for example that brewery ad which tries to persuade us that modern man drinks beer. If all this is our dream of modernisation, then we had better wake up quickly because, for us, it is not within the realm of possibility. Even if it were possible, it would bring disaster to each and every Indonesian and lead our society up a blind alley as it has done the rich, industrial, progressive nations.

Think about these statistics. At present 1/3 of the people living in luxury-orientated, progressive, industrial nations consume 3/4 of the crops harvested in the world. Agricultural science and technology were developed in these rich nations. In the United States the farmer actually receives a subsidy for not planting certain crops in order to maintain high market prices. In that country people throw food away while in other countries people are starving. Ironically, we don't talk much about the fate of human beings. We get used to not practising what we preach.

All of this is reflected in our language. It would be very interesting, for example, to conduct an examination of the Indonesian pattern of reactions to various incidents, words and symbols. S.I. Hayakawa calls this reaction pattern 'semantic habits'. Usually semantics and vocabularies are accumulations of all of our education, both good and bad, beginning with parental influence since earliest childhood. Our education includes all that they taught us, all of our formal education and all of the lectures, speeches and conversations we have heard. It also takes in radio, TV, movies, books, newspapers, picture books, magazines, all conversations with our friends and acquaintances and draws from all of our experiences.

The dictionary defines semantics as the science of the meaning of words. Hayakawa agrees that this definition is satisfactory provided we do not consider that looking for the meaning of words begins and ends in the dictionary. Semantics is not looking for the meaning of words which are made clearer by using other words. As Nobel Prize Winner Bridgeman, a nuclear expert, wrote, 'A word's meaning can be found only in examining what a person does with that word and not what he says with it.' For example, if I say that this table weighs 30 kilograms, then what I say can be proven on a scale. If I say that I am six foot tall, you could measure me. But, if I say that I am going to establish the 'rule of law', or develop people's values or human independence, or that I am going to create a *Pancasila* society with equal prosperity and justice for all, or claim that in our country we have a responsible free press, how would you measure or investigate the truth of what I say? You cannot measure it with a scale or meter.

Here is another illustration. An executive examined a job application. Under 'education', the applicant had written LL.B. The executive immediately threw the application into the wastebasket. He was turned off by the symbol L L.B., because in his opinion an LL.B. was worthless. He had a semantic reaction to the words and toward the sign and slogan. He displayed a human response to language.

According to Hayakawa a basic premise of semantics is that the meanings of words and symbols are not found in the words themselves, but rather in our semantic reactions to those words.

How do people respond to the words: *Pancasila*, democracy, new order, Ampera, Tritura, abolition of corruption, justice, freedom, rights of man, rule of law, police, public prosecutor, judge, director general, minister, general, top executive and oil? Upon reading or hearing these words do people react by discarding the newspapers they are reading or turning off the radios and TVs to which they are listening? ·

Will Indonesians continue as a people of mantras, slogans and symbols or as a people who can accomplish and create things? Will we remain a nation of people who play with words which eventually cease to have any meaning for both speaker and listener? Again, I leave it to you.

Fifth Characteristic

A fifth prime characteristic of the Indonesian is that he is artistic. Because his life is closely attuned to the spirit, the soul and the supernatural power of things around him, the Indonesian is virtually united with nature. He lives by instinct, feelings and sensuality, all of which develop an astute artistic ability. This ability is demonstrated in all sorts of beautiful creations and handicrafts which the artist produces in a multitude of forms, colours, and variations. For hundreds of years right up to present times, Indonesian artistic creations have been going out of our country. Museums in the United States, Europe and other countries proudly collect our copper work, weaving, batik, stone sculptures and wood carvings — Lampung, Batak Toraja and Sumba weavings, Balinese carvings and intricate gold and silver work from the Moluccas and Kalimantan.

Our music, dancing and folklore reveal the rich and fertile imagination of our people which inspires our tremendous creativity. To me the artistic character of Indonesians is the most interesting and fascinating of all. It is both a resource and a focus for the future of Indonesia.

Sixth Characteristic

The sixth Indonesian characteristic is an indecisive disposition. Many an Indonesian lacks strength in defending and fighting for his beliefs. He is rash and will abandon his convictions if put under pressure. In this personality we can clearly observe the symptoms of the prostitution of our society.

Such behaviour occurred during Soekarno's reign of madness, when he disregarded all scientific principles in order to achieve his 'revolution', and again during the Japanese occupation. Soekarno once said that inflation was good as long as it promoted the Indonesian revolution. At the time he fell from power our country's rate of inflation had reached 650% per annum. Our nation was bankrupt and our populace disorganised. During those years, when Soekarno commented on the value of inflation, our economic experts applauded and approved our great revolutionary leader's brilliant idea. There was also an economist then who praised Marxist principles (of which he himself was not convinced), but later when Soekarno fell this same economist spoke highly of the 'free market' economy — a way to avoid saying capitalist economy.

During the Japanese occupation the late Dr. Prijono[1] allowed himself to be exploited. He put together a propaganda booklet for the Japanese Army to use in their deception of the Indonesians. The professor wrote for a military publication ...... 'The Emperor feels toward the people as a father feels toward his children. A father would truly seek happiness and safety for his children not only with kind words but with sincere honest feelings borne out in his character and behaviour...' Prijono continued that throughout the history of Japan, which goes back 2604 years, no Japanese emperor or nobleman had ever used his authority to oppress the people or to attain his selfish desires as had sometimes happened in other countries, especially in Europe, and also in Asia.

This is totally false. The Japanese authors themselves have written quite extensively about the abuse of power by various Japanese rulers. A main theme is the use of samurai terror tactics against the people in the nobility's struggle for power. A scholar of Dr. Prijono's calibre should have known better than to have produced such a fabrication.

Characteristic instability such as Dr. Prijono displayed is a product of our feudal society. It presents another side of the ABS mentality — keeping those in power happy while saving one's own skin. For keeping Indonesians happy today we

---

1 Early nationalist who held various high government positions including that of Minister of Education.

32

have a new outlook called *tepo sliro* [knowing one's place]. It is no different, however, and creates instability on both sides — the strong and the weak.

Other Characteristics

With regard to other characteristics, let me start with another of the undesirable ones. The Indonesian is wasteful. He is not an 'economic animal'. As a matter of fact he is very good at spending money he has not yet received, or which he never will receive. He is inclined to be extravagant. He enjoys dressing well, displaying his finery and partying. Today this tendency is manifested in luxurious houses, cars, big parties, exclusive use of foreign-made products, playing golf — in short, anything which indicates wealth.

Today's Indonesian shuns work except when necessary. There is a tendency now for everyone to aspire to become an instant millionaire — much as Americans make instant tea. He wants so much to get an academic degree that the Indonesian is willing to forge or buy a diploma which will in turn lead to his promotion to a higher level and eventually put him in a position that will enable him to get rich.

Becoming a white-collar worker or a civil servant is the Indonesian's goal because goverment affiliation is such an important status symbol to him. People do not become civil servants because of any desire to serve the common people, or to help society progress. Officials, both high and low, do not want to be transferred from Java or from large cities. We now even have symbolic terms to describe the locations of jobs: *kering* vs. *basah* and *kurus* vs. *gemuk* [hard vs. easy money-making locations].

With few exceptions there is currently a lack of interest in entering private business. As a matter of fact, what the Indonesian is striving for today is to become a composite of three P's: 1) to be a *penguasa* [a man of power within the government], 2) to moonlight as a *pengusaha* [a business man], and 3) where possible to have *pengetahuan* [to be knowledgeable in what he does]. These three P's are our present ideal. This pattern in the relationship between the government and the entrepreneur existed in our culture before the advent of the Dutch East India Company. During the Dutch rule it was further strengthened when the colonisers cooperated with the Chinese businessmen rather than the native merchants.

The younger generation is no exception. They all want to get rich quick, have high-ranking positions, be top-notch journalists, famous authors, well-known artists, champions of this or champions of that. They want to accomplish this with no pain and very little effort.

Our people have become much less patient. The complainer has become a common character in our society. He is not, however, brave enough to complain openly, but only in his home or among those friends who are sympathetic to his feelings.

The Indonesian is also jealous of those who seem to be more successful than he is. He looks unhappily on those who have progressed farther, are richer, have a higher position, have more power, are brighter and are more famous. The result here is the emergence of the 'cheap detective'. He appears on every street corner, and his reports are used to bring about the downfall of those whom his employers dislike or of whom they are suspicious.

When men and women are chosen to be included on a list

34

of best-dressed people they are very proud. At the same time they know that such a choice is without any basis at all. There are 130 million people in Indonesia and say half of them are adults. How could it be possible to choose from so many those who are best dressed? But the winners are proud and happy to be famous. Such vanity is meaningless.

Pearls of wisdom are to be found in Indonesian ethnic literature, in our ancient philosophy and culture. It is a pity that such wisdom has been ignored. Ki Hadjar Dewantara[1] never tired of saying:

It is better to live as a syrup vendor, but happy,
Than as a rich man, but suffering.

Who wants to hear Ki Hadjar Dewantara now? Doesn't our slogan today advise, 'You would be a fool to waste an opportunity. If you don't take it now, then when?'

Once a minister told me that today's philosophy is that of *kebeneran* [to be in the inner circle, in the right place at the right time]. Even if you are *benar* [correct], but not *kebeneran*, then you will be considered wrong. On the other hand, if you are wrong, but *kebeneran*, you will be considered right.

The Indonesian can also be said to be easily carried away with his success. If he has power, he easily becomes drunk with it. If he is rich, he becomes drunk with wealth and greed. To be specific, take the case of the *Dolog*[2] in Kalimantan. When he was at the height of his glory, he became cocky and

---

1 Founder of the Taman Siswa educational system which emphasised that students learn about their Indonesian heritage.
2 Refers to Budiadji, a chief, who was prosecuted for the embezzlement of six billion rupiahs.

acted as though he were the most extraordinary man in the world.

The Indonesian is also a copier. His individuality is weak, and he copies any foreigner who catches his fancy. Many Indonesians became whining cowboys when this American prototype was in style, and others became wistful hippies when it was the season for flower children. Outside influences have a strong effect on us. Imported products are always more appealing than our own.

I feel that we must be honest in admitting that the Indonesian possesses various undesirable traits. He can be cruel, fail to control his temper, run amok, commit murder, arson, treason, oppress others, blackmail, deceive, steal, be corrupt, malicious, hypocritical. In bringing out these miserable characteristics I feel that the Indonesian appears no better or worse than peoples of other nations in the world.

The Indonesian's traits which differ from other peoples' are an inclination toward laziness because of his natural surroundings, living only from day to day, and a laxity in saving for tomorrow or giving much consideration to the future. However, to say that the Indonesian lacks an understanding of practical things is untrue, as may be seen in this Malay proverb:

berdendang biduk hilir,
sedang berdiang nasi masak.

Going downstream on a boat we sing,
Warming our bodies while cooking.

The Indonesian is logical enough. If we study the adages of our ancestors we see that their thinking was indeed sharp and logical. It is because his animistic beliefs weaken his scientific inquiry that the Indonesian ends up applying his logic to the wrong premises. For example, when Mt. Merapi erupts the Indonesian believes the gods are angry and he must make offerings to quieten the active volcano. In an eclipse he must beat a large drum, a pregnant woman must hide under her bed, and incantations must be chanted and then the sun will reappear. If there is an epidemic it is because demons or other evil spirits are angry, and again the Indonesian makes placatory offerings. The problem here is not that the Indonesian lacks logic, but the premises on which he bases his conclusions are wrong. Cause and effect are confused. Our society is still influenced by left-over attitudes, and they make us slow to understand the relationship between cause and effect.

This is all reinforced by an acquiescent attitude — belief in predestination, in fate, that God has predetermined everything. This attitude discourages logic and breeds defeatism. Thus, if the people suffer from a yearly flood, they will merely heave a sigh and piously accept the trials put upon them by God Almighty. Only a few people take into account the possibility that the flooding might be the result of mistakes or carelessness on the part of those whose duty it is to protect and clean the estuary, river and dike.

Another Indonesian characteristic is the attitude of 'I don't much care what happens to others as long as it doesn't affect me or those close to me.' A person looks upon himself as uninvolved, and as such, a disinterested party. It is as though he lacks a real interest in anyone else's existence. We can see this in practice. It is not unusual for the authorities to arrest someone and detain him for a long time before bringing him to trial. When the detainee finally appears in court the judge may decide to drop the whole matter, neglecting to take into account the fact that the man has already spent time in jail.

There is no way the detainee can touch the official responsible for his false arrest.

Some men, especially in the Indonesian bureaucracy, are so entrenched in the bureaucratic system that they seem to have lost all interest in humanity. If by contrast, however, a petitioner knows an official personally, or he is a friend or relative, then the bureaucrat can be understanding and change the situation completely.

If we look at the real characterisitcs of the Indonesian people, we will see that this lack of concern for others has not always been the case. The Indonesian society is one that developed from rice cultivation which required an elaborate irrigation system that had to be both regulated and protected and which consequently called for great cooperation. There was mutual aid, everyone looking out for everyone else with all of society's structures rooted in the tribe. The tribes subscribed to exogamous marriage systems (marriage was strictly forbidden within the tribe). Because marriage was based on the exchange of men and women between tribes, more intimate tribal relationships were fostered. The foundation of the tribal intermarriage system kept our ancient society from developing a power centre, simply because each tribe wanted to retain its own autonomy.

With the advent of Hinduism, feudalism got a big boost. Hinduism brought in a more regulated life-style, 'sociocosmic dualism', a relationship between micro and macro cosmos. In the macrocosmos the god Indra was in the centre flanked by four other gods located at the four points of the compass. They were surrounded in turn by thirty-two other gods. Hindu-Javanese society reflected this macrocosmos by placing the king's palace in the centre of the grounds. The kind (who held the power of a worldly god) was in the palace flanked by four ministers and thirty-two officials from all corners of the country.

When Islam was introduced, Hindu-Javanese feudalism changed very little. The Javanese king, who represented God, remained in the centre of the society, but was now given the title of Sultan and the additional title of *Khalifahtullah*, implying that he held a mandate from God. Thus the Islamic kings, in Java and elsewhere, were also sacred. There was no real change from the previous era.

Deep in the Indonesian's soul, however, there still exists a concern for others. For example, when the newspaper *Indonesia Raya* asked for contributions to aid a Chinese youth who had had hydrochloric acid thrown in his face, the response was tremendous. Within a short time several million rupiahs poured into the editor's office. When the paper wrote about a student who could not walk because of a severe beating, a generous Indonesian donated a wheel chair to him and Merpati Airlines flew the chair and a reporter to Kutaraja at no charge. Social agencies and newspapers could cite many more similar examples.

Another characteristic basic to our Indonesian culture is the love of parents for their children and vice versa. This love, as long as it is not overshadowed by one's outside interests, is a fragile Indonesian value which we must maintain. The Indonesian is basically soft-hearted and peace-loving. He also has a good sense of humour and is able to laugh in the face of trouble and suffering. The Indonesian is observant and quick to learn. He is easily trained in those skills requiring the use of his hands. He is also a man of unbounded patience, which can sometimes be a fault. Therefore, besides the ugly face which I have drawn, it is also true that the Indonesian possesses model qualities which can be further developed.

After we have gazed at our reflection to our satisfaction, let's see if what we observe in the mirror compares with our own view of ourselves as Indonesians. Our personalities, characteristics, attitudes and values are all moulded by the surrounding society and various symbols. These influences result in an Indonesian who shows one face to the world and another, which he often denies, to himself. For example, a man of power likes to appear as a servant of the people, a lover of the common man, a supporter of human freedom and the rule of law, honest, and in favour of all things which are good for the general welfare of the people. But suppose this leader is actually malicious, selfish, power-hungry, egotistical and cowardly, he would certainly not want the public to see this undesirable side of his personality. Many people manage to hide such vices so that others are unaware of them. Such a person's actions and attitudes, however, will be influenced by both faces, whether or not he denies or suppresses one of them.

Let us start our comparison with the ideal Indonesian according to the Javanese philosophy. One of the main goals in life here is to follow the principle: 'Hard work with no thought of profit will better the world.' This is personified in the wise knight, people who have already controlled their own *jagag cilik* and themselves, the commander who acts as a dispenser of wisdom, the scholar who understands the secret of life — man's beginning and end — and those who live in the world and yet continue to consider themselves apart from it. Thus, the pure man goes through life as a divine messenger, indeed a great messenger of God. This is an Indonesian face which clearly does not agree with what we have been scrutinising in the mirror. It is actually a face of man that appears only in dreams — one he will never truly achieve. It is an ideal which is unattainable.

Man is shaped by his surroundings, his society, the nature of his life, various standards encouraged by society, the people in his community, education, and models which are picked up at school, at home and from friends. Can people exist in the great world and still dominate their own small worlds while from day to day they face all sorts of persuasive influences such as a thousand Chinese merchants who offer chests of money and gold, bank accounts everywhere, Mercedes Benz 350s or Rolls Royces? Such influences could also include a woman in Hong Kong, New York, Paris, or Geneva; 'cooperation' from multi-national businesses; luxury homes with imported Italian marble floors; thousands of hectares of land with livestock; golf with the international jet-set; waves of advertising and commercial propaganda; and international consumerism which comes to us through the press, radio, TV, and movies and which spreads from the large cities into the interior areas, the mountains and the valleys.

How can people change themselves if their society does not change, if their values do not change and if their aspirations are not fulfilled? In short, if our feudal, semi-feudal, and neo-feudal societies, with all the attending characteristics which I have mentioned, are not consciously altered, then it will not be possible for the Indonesian to change and develop, to become a man of strong personality and character with the values and attitudes which he needs to face today's world and to save his country so that it might continue to prosper in the next century. With fluctuating personalities, as well as all the characteristics we saw reflected earlier, I am seriously concerned that our people will be left behind. What is more unfortunate is that we will become victims in the development of the modern world.

Our syncretic upbringing, which is partly caused by 'knowing one's placc', means that we easily accept all sorts of paradoxes which have ambiguous meanings. We do not like to look at each other's opposing characteristics, but are inclined to look for each other's complementary characteristics. As a result we feel happy and comfortable discussing one thing and later doing the opposite of what we just said. We accept all sorts of things which are contradictory. For example, we say that we obey the rule of law, but at the same time we blithely break it. This is reflected in our languages, especially Javanese and Sundanese which have honorific levels, etc. In other ethnic groups this is reflected in such feudal anachronisms as: 'My Lord ... His Majesty ... Your slave,' and also in colours and clothing which are reserved exclusively for royalty.

Our language has already absorbed words which were used during the Japanese occupation to address the emperor or Japanese military leaders. Take for example the word *berkenan*, which literally means 'to be pleased' but came to be used only when referring to people of higher levels. Thus we would say, 'The Emperor *berkenan* to announce this or that,' or 'The high military official *berkenan* with this or that.' We go blindly on still using such words. Now, the president *berkenan* to open such and such a factory or the minister *berkenan* to open a conference, as if the leaders who are carrying out their duties and obligations were doing their jobs as favours or out of kindness and generosity for the people.

The very use of these words alone has a damaging effect on our understanding of the relationship between the governor and the governed in the democratic society which we are trying to establish. In the use of Indonesian we now see reflected our dislike and fear of clarity and openness. We no longer 'raise' but now 'adjust' a price. A newspaper wrote in large-type headlines about a non-bloc, high-level conference in Colombo: ACCOMPLISHMENTS NOT DISAPPOINT-ING BUT NOT SATISFACTORY EITHER.

We are diligent in asking a VIP for his blessing in anything that we do.

We have changed the word prison to Rehabilitation Centre. In practice we have only made a new empty symbol. Ah, how beautiful are the words 'Rehabilitation Centre'. It is as though, while in there, those evaders of the law and wrong-doers are undergoing a rehabilitation process for educating them to return to the outside world as good and useful members of society. But is that what actually happens? There is no rehabilitation process during detention in our prisons. Prisons, or Rehabilitation Centres, are one and the same, and as such form a cadre for performing all sorts of evil doings. Apprentice pickpockets, leaving the prison in four or four-teen months, become superior pickpockets. A burglar or robber comes out with new technology and more skill. The con man will be more clever and deceitful. We have, there-fore, only changed a name and not done anything to fulfill the promise of that new name. Nothing has been done to encourage the inmates to become good citizens and thus be more useful to themselves and to society. We have not created a new and fresh climate in our prisons and we have totally failed to present the convicts with any new oppor-tunities for self-improvement. On the contrary, the prisons of the free and *Pancasila*-orientated Indonesia are more foul than they were during the Dutch colonial period. This holds true whether one is talking about food, treatment, or atten-tion to detainees or prisoners. We sorely need reform and change in this matter.

Under the Dutch Colonial Civil Service, when the wind of

Holland's ethics blew strong, a moral attitude was urged based on ethical values for serving society and government. The ideal was once again the Javanese slogan, 'Work hard with no thought of profit and the world will become better.' The Dutch awarded yearly gold and silver stars to loyal and hard-working civil servants. Besides these civil servants, however, there was another group whose members were also products of Dutch education and learning. Although they too went through the Dutch educational system, they were disliked by the colonials and were classified by the Dutch Secret Police as half-wits, sly dogs, reprobates, and argumentative and quarrelsome brawlers. This group included people like Soekarno, Hatta, Sjahrir, Mangunkusumo, Ki Hadjar Dewantara, and thousands of others who were exiled to Boven Digul and Tanah Merah and other remote places.

Nowadays, in addition to the Communist Party, those who are considered the people's enemies are those who are labelled as the 'new left', 'subversives', those who oppose law and order, those who disturb peace and security, and international humanists. This attitude encourages the 'cheap detectives' to go on making their ABS reports.

The names change and the symbols change, but in actuality little else changes. We are still chained by the old fetters, but with a new label. As a result we are incapable of looking ahead to the future, and we lack a clear perception of what is happening in the world around us. We are still unsure of what national goals we wish to pursue, apart from the casting of abstract slogans like *Pancasila* society, *Pancasila* men, etc. We remain tied to our mantras and symbols. We are either spellbound or weary, but powerless to face up to expressions like 'common people ... people's struggle ... spirit of the 45 revolution ... independence ... sovereignty of the common people ... freedom of mankind ... glory of mankind ... human rights ... justice ... prosperity for all ... *Pancasila* democracy ... unity ... freedom of expression.'

We are confused in using words like *bapak*, *ibu* [mother, respected woman], *bung* [brother, friend], *abang* [elder brother], *kakak* [older sibling], *oom* [uncle], and *tante* [aunt]. To call our superior *bung* is now considered disrespectful. We must use *bapak*, although the VIP has just turned twenty and the speaker addressing is over sixty. *Saudara* [relative, friend] and *bung* were popular words spoken proudly during our struggle for freedom and through the revolutionary years. In the past ten or twenty years, however, they have come to be considered no longer respectful forms of address. Is it possible to save the Indonesian language from all sorts of jargon, symbols, futility, staleness, impreciseness, evil, and disorganised semantics?

The higher-ups are patronising and authoritarian toward their subordinates. In public Indonesians use masks to hide their true identities. They are anxious and terrified to strip off these masks simply because underneath are their ugly, frightening, real faces — which scare even themselves!

Granted, we are unafraid to face reality and admit to a slackening of our revolutionary spirit of 1945. That spirit has weakened and almost vanished from our society. The national spirit which once united both important and common people was one which drove us all with the same urgency. It lightened the load we carried. It was a spirit filled with bravery and a willingness to sacrifice our lives if necessary for the independence of our country. The sacredness of the struggle, the willingness to forget individual as well as group interests, the readiness to overlook jealousies and prejudices in order to fight for our own power, the desire to gather as much national wealth as possible in the shortest time, the spirit of mutual aid and give-and-take are now weak and dying.

Our élite live happy, comfortable and luxurious lives. They wear the clothes of Paris designers like Yves St. Laurent, Dior, Blamain, Nina Ricci, Balenciaga and Cardin. Their shirts, jackets and other attire are from Paris, London and New York, and their shoes are from Rome. They take vacations in Nice, France, Mexico and Switzerland, and they go on safari in Kenya. We have long since abandoned the old, worn-out cars that we were once delighted to have and that we gave such tender loving care to during the revolutionary years. Ordinary cars are no longer good enough for us. We must now drive Mercedes 350s, Rolls Royces or Cadillacs. Lately, championed by the 'haves', we have begun to enjoy playing golf, and we give golf prizes to the Japanese, for example. We even hear stories of Indonesians who have mansions on the Costa Brava, in Florida, San Francisco, Hong Kong, Singapore and Amsterdam.

We also hear of Indonesians who own race horses in Paris and London and of other countrymen who gamble in Las Vegas and lose tens of thousands or even hundreds of thousands of dollars in one night without batting an eye. They merely smile and play again the next day. We hear of Indonesians who keep mistresses in foreign countries where they set them up in luxurious apartments with all sorts of expensive clothes, jewels and cars.

Year by year we allow our élite to increase their riches and continue their corruption, robbing the people of Indonesia of their rights and wealth. Take for example what happened with the oil company Pertamina, the tin company PN Timah, Dolog Kalimantan, and several others which have as yet remained uncovered. Our élite pretend to lead but their way of life cuts them off from the people, and communication between the two groups becomes more difficult every day.

We do not understand the importance of time — something that will never come back once it is gone. For us time is always there. Our attitude toward time is: why do it today if you can do it tomorrow? We certainly are slow, but not necessarily sure.

One of our popular new words is *dalang* [puppeteer, mastermind]. When there is a student protest it is followed by the accusation, 'Who is the *dalang*?' or, 'Surely it was masterminded.' If a wave of criticism appears in the press, the same question is soon asked, 'Who is the *dalang*?' This is also true in many other instances: if something does not please a certain group, then that thing must have been masterminded. We do not seem to believe that our students can think for themselves, gather information and collect their own data, make their own assessments draw their own conclusions and decide on a course of action. Aren't universities established and developed to make young people think?

According to the experts' statistics, during the last ten years as much as 200 billion rupiahs domestic capital (U.S.$4.5 billion) and an additional 850 foreign investments (U.S.$6.5 billion) have been invested in Indonesia. With all of this investment capital we have only been able to create 1.2 million jobs. In our country every year 1.1 million people enter the job market looking for work. We must fully grasp the implication of this development.

Gandhi once said, 'The earth provides enough for everyone's need, but not enough for everyone's greed.' Oh, how true the late Gandhi's words of warning are. If we were to fulfill our desire to have a high standard of living, with cars, TVs, electronic equipment, lavish food, all sorts of luxuries in abundance, telephones in every room, air-conditioners and central heating, electric toothbrushes, shoe polishers, hair clippers, power saws, etc., then all the raw materials in the world would not be sufficient for our requirements. That route is a dead-end street. It would mean that we would have to compete for raw materials with the rich countries: the industrial, economic and military giants. We can never even dream of being able to compete with them for natural resources. We must use our intelligence to look for other means of happiness, peace, and vitalising our country.

If an Indonesian sits on the shore and looks out at the Southern Sea what goes on in his head? Is it an image of Nyai Loro Kidul [legendary queen of the South Sea], or is it thoughts of the riches of the sea waiting to be mined? For the latter we must control science and technology, but we must be careful. Science is powerful, and power is never neutral. Are science and technology neutral? Or do many scientists say this in order to preserve their own peace of mind and accuse those who use science and technology for purposes of war, such as the production of all sorts of terrifying weapons. These weapons vary from gases which affect the nerves or which stay in the atmosphere and continue to kill people, to bacterial or viral warfare, to chemicals which cause the leaves to fall from trees thus killing the trees and wiping out the jungles (such as the defoliants used by the American military forces in Vietnam). Science and technology which do not have positive uses can ruin a society.

People in ages past controlled technology cleverly. During the reign of Ptolemy, in Egypt, a steam engine was developed for pumping water to the top of a lighthouse on Pharos Island. Not long after its installation they stopped using it. It was thought that it made people lazy and unwilling to work. This also happened with a mechanised wheel that the Romans used to grind wheat.

We now claim that we want to create jobs, but at the same time we allow the entry of foreign capital which brings with it a capital-intensive technology.

Several years ago a speaker in Cibulan said that man's ultimate goal is to serve God. He claimed that God created both men and demons to serve Him. What is the nature of this service to God? Is it merely attendance at church or mosque? Do we obey all the laws and fulfill all the obligations of our religions?

We must learn to be far-sighted and carefully control the exploitation of our natural resources, our capital, our manpower, science and technology, so as not to upset our country's ecological balance and thereby cause an environmental disaster. We must realise that people's freedom can only develop if there are people who are brave enough to want to be free. The sky must always be the limit for opportunity, chance and new prospects for Indonesians.

Some time ago Chris Siner Key (a former leader of the Catholic Students' Association) described students as: apathetic, hazy and disorientated; without vision or motivation; lacking idealism and spiritual values; unimaginative and uncreative; uncapable of logical and critical thinking. He said that these faults were caused by fear, frustration and the feeling of the students that they were always too closely watched and controlled. Doesn't this description fit not only the students but also our society in general?

Christians look to the teachings of Christ for salvation. The Bible teaches that Christ, not man, is the centre of everything, and a world without Christ is meaningless. Christians believe that all have sinned and must pay for their sins.

Islam teaches that peace in this world and the world hereafter is achieved through service and obedience to Allah's laws and those of His Prophet Mohammed. One must bow to the will of Almighty God.

Time, in Javanese thinking, is circular, returning repeatedly like a wheel turning full circle. The new is also old, and the old is also new. Because of this philosophy, people still look to the *wayang* stories which were written thousands of years ago as priceless links with the wisdom of the past.

Tonight we must not speak too much of religion, because it leads us to many other sensitive topics, and also because we can never agree. Each religion claims to be the true one.

But whatever our religion, we have to admit that, since independence, a gap has appeared and has been widening between our national pretensions based on *Pancasila*, and our individual as well as our group behaviour.

Today's World

A sign of the times today is the ever-widening gap between the rich industrial nations and the poor developing ones. Various economic indicators of western origin are used to determine which countries are developed and which are underdeveloped or developing. This method of assessment gives a false impression; it leads many people into believing that rich countries are more advanced in all fields of civilisation and culture, and that developing countries are inferior in all respects.

If we compare values outside the economic sector, we will see that many cultural and social values in the less-developed societies are superior to those in the developed ones.

Do we want to be like Japan, the United States and the Western European countries, or like the U.S.S.R. and Communist China? In progressive, rich countries like America, Japan and Western Europe there are many clear-thinking people who would like to see their societies do an about-face and abandon the pursuit of profit and materialism. The world has already been brought to the brink of disaster by the ruthless consumption of its natural resources, the disruption of the ecological balance and the poisoning of our surroundings by technological giants, machines, computers, automation and robotisation, all of which have caused man to fall from his place in the centre of universe. He has become just an unimportant appendage and button-pusher for all types of machines and electronic tools. Today these tools determine the life or death of the technologically advanced societies. They defeat human considerations and rob mankind of the right to determine its own fate. Maintaining or increasing Gross National Products or Gross Domestic Products has become the main aim of both the developed as well as the developing countries. How primitive and backward such thinking is!

These attitudes are rooted, among other things, in the doctrine of Francis Bacon, one of the founders of modern science. Bacon said that the ultimate aim of science was to lead man to new discoveries and enrich his life. He further said that man must be the conqueror, not the conquered, of the world.

In developed countries, with technology which demands all sorts of calculation processes — to predict future trends, to gather and disseminate data, to execute and supervise production, etc. — things must be done more efficiently, more expediently and more economically. According to this mode of thinking, man is not only a mere subsystem within the whole system, but he is also the most ineffective part of the system. He is the most inclined to make mistakes and have shortcomings. In brief, he is not 'foolproof' like the machines and electronic equipment available today.

He has the ability to remember vast amounts of data, but his abilities are inferior to those of a computer when it comes to organising data, processing it speedily and recalling it accurately.

Man's position in the world is already slipping. The symptoms can be seen in the societies of several progressive countries. Feelings of apprehension, doubt, unhappiness, extreme isolation and the weakening of intimate relationships between a person and his family cause many of these people to yearn for and to seek other values and to look to other societies for spiritual fulfillment.

In the United States *gurus* from India have come to be very popular. Everywhere we go we see young men and women with shaved heads dressed in yellow cotton robes. They dance while beating drums and chanting, *'Hare Krishna! Hare Krishna!'* Also popular is the Transcendental Meditation theory of Mahareshi Yogi, who distributes mantras at a price in excess of $100 each. This philosophy has spread throughout the world, even to Indonesia, as if here, too, the sick symptoms of the rich societies have caused many Indonesians to develop all sorts of doubts, fears, high-blood pressure and the inability to find contentment. The Pak Subud retreat in Cilandak is filled with foreigners who come here looking for tranquillity and inner peace.

The experts from the countries with extensive scientific knowledge and modern and powerful technology now come here and tell us that the problems which we face, such as overpopulation, poverty, disruption of the ecology, education, etc., can be overcome through technology. Technology can solve them all. Overpopulation can be taken care of by the pill, IUDs and condoms. As a matter of fact, it is currently claimed that there is a kind of vaccination to prevent pregnancy, and, if all else fails, non-surgical safe abortions can now be performed. A new technique has already been discovered, using an instrument which sucks the foetus from the mother's uterus.

Many people now believe that technology is the key to modernisation. If we fail to acquire modern technology, then we cannot enter the modern age. Again, we must clearly define the meaning of modernisation for the sake of our country and our society. Is modernisation something which can only be reflected in the latest technological equipment, like computers, giant steel factories, rockets, etc., or by modernisation should we mean rational thought, and minds which are always striving to seek realistic and total solutions to mankind's problems? Perhaps the demand to discard various technologies, which can now be perceived as ecologically damaging and wasting the world's natural resources, will be considered a modern attitude in the next ten to twenty years.

An example close to all of us is the automobile. The carbon monoxide emitted from a running car in a closed garage can be lethal. In addition to this danger, the amount of carbon dioxide in the air increases every year, and it is predicted that in time it will alter the pattern of the world's climate.

We once considered things like automotive technology

development as extremely helpful in solving the problem of transporting people and things. Possibly in twenty years it will be in vogue to demand that trees no longer be cut for lumber and jungles no longer be arbitrarily cleared. In many sections of the world where jungles have been destroyed the results have been disastrous. Pouring rains have brought floods, soil erosion, etc. This has already happened on Java. We do know, however, that the very technology which permits large-scale jungle clearing helps people find work, encourages the lumber industry, the lumber-shipping companies, and the construction companies. We see, therefore, that technology can solve one problem, but sometimes creates another more serious than the first. The pollution of the Great Lakes in the United States is a good example. The industries surrounding the lakes have carelessly spread their wastes and poisoned these waters, killing the life within them. This has also happened to the river Rhine in Western Europe and in various places in Russia and Japan. This is why in the long run a piecemeal application of technology to our problems is not only inefficient but also ineffective and the results can be more dangerous and more destructive than the problems. The outcome does not affect just one place, one city, or one group in society, but our entire world.

What happens in one section of the world will affect another. Yet no country has based its internal and foreign policies, its way of life, its goals and its values on the concept of what is best for the world instead of merely the nation. Poor countries want to grow rich and rich countries want to get richer.

When the Arabs implemented their oil boycott against the United States and the Western European countries in order to urge them to become more active in seeking a solution to the Palestinian problem that was fair to the Arabs, many

Americans realised just how dependent their prosperity and happiness were upon the oil producers in the developing countries. This led them to become more prudent in their use of oil. For example, in the United States cars were not allowed to travel faster than 55 miles per hour and people were urged to join car pools to save petrol. Less heat was used in large buildings and homes, unnecessary lights were turned off and other fuel-saving measures were taken. As soon as the Arabs called off the boycott people forgot all about this. The number of automobiles in the United States, Western Europe and Japan increased tremendously. On the main German freeways there is now no speed limit. In the industrial countries oil consumption continues to climb.

In 1976 America imported 42% of its necessary oil, and in 1977 the need for imported oil will increase to 46%. Throughout the rich countries oil use continues to increase, with consumption in the U.S. climbing the fastest.

Inflation and/or unemployment are rampant throughout the world. Everywhere the prices of manufactured goods are increasing from 8% to over 10%. But, as soon as the OPEC countries said that they planned to raise the price of gasoline, a great war of nerves was waged against the oil-producing nations, and the rich countries protested that the 10% or more rise in oil prices was without foundation. They said that this move would hamper the restoration of the development of their economies and as a result the rich countries would be unable to help the poor countries. The United States was successful in its attempt to break the alignment of poor countries with the OPEC nations. In the end the United Arab Emirates and Saudi Arabia subscribed to a different policy from other OPEC members'.

A Dutch newspaper told of Dutch housewives who, in

1973, threw out more than 79,000 tons of bread and in America 100,000,000 loaves, at 53¢ a loaf, were discarded. How many hundreds of thousands of tons of food are thrown away? If the amount of meat, fish, bread, etc. thrown out in enormously rich societies like Japan, Western Europe, and the United States were known, we would all be astounded.

When I was in Holland last year, a Dutch man questioned me about my opinion of OPEC's plan to raise oil prices.

'What if it ends up disturbing the rich countries' development?' he asked.

'That's all right,' I answered.

He looked at me in amazement.

I told him, 'On the contrary, it will be good for you and the world if OPEC raised oil prices so that oil becomes even more expensive to burn than it is now. If you had ten or even twenty per cent less wealth it would not be a disaster for you, and if oil is too expensive to burn, then the whole world will look for a new energy source, like the sun, ocean tides, wind, geothermal energy, etc., and oil would be used in the production of other things more valuable to mankind.'

The quality of life for these people would not decline if each family had only one TV set, or one telephone, instead of telephones in almost every room, even in the bathroom and kitchen. There should also be just one car per family rather than two or three, and new models need not be purchased every year.

This brings us back to the necessity of defining for ourselves what is meant by 'economic progress'. Do we want economic progress as it is defined by the rich countries today with all the attending negative aspects and disasters which seem to occur to people, nature, society and man's values? Or is economic progress for us a desire to have no Indonesians hungry, enough housing for all, a chance for every child to go to school and study either formally or informally, suitable job opportunities for all and a guarantee that birth and death will not become luxuries beyond our means?

If the initial aim of our economic development is to fill the minimum requirements of nutritious food, adequate clothing, satisfactory housing, appropriate jobs and equal educational opportunities for everyone, then the list of our priorities is more modest than that of the rich countries. The capital and technology which we wish to mobilise would also be different from that which we would need to imitate and pursue the 'economic development' of the wealthy nations.

Perhaps we should concentrate our interests and capital investments in villages or interior areas. Expanding agricultural industries means the development of small industries making all sorts of farming tools, improvement of seedlings and organic fertiliser, tackling insects and plant diseases by using more vegetable-based substances and by all these means increasing the production of food mainly, like rice, corn, beans, vegetables, fresh and salt water fish and fruit. This would not be just for us to eat, but also for export.

With the decrease of available farm land in various parts of the world, due to industrialisation and the increase of the world's population, food production will be a vital industry in the future. Given the incentive and the leadership along with the appropriate technology, Indonesia, with her fertile land and with her tradition of an agriculturally orientated people, could become one of the most important food-producing countries in the world. The industrial-agricultural sector of our economy is one which we must never disregard; in fact, it should be given first priority in our economic development. It is said that 100,000,000 people will suffer from hunger in the next twenty-five years. If things continue as they are, 100,000 people could die of starvation every day. I do not see any reason why Indonesia could not produce her own food, and even export some.

Furthermore, we can use other types of modern technology to meet our needs. For example, our requirement of steel for the construction of bridges, housing, large buildings, automobiles, trucks, trains, and airplanes, among other things, should not encourage us to build a steel factory. Technology has already produced new materials which are cheaper and do not require the heavy equipment needed to produce steel. Man can now produce material just as good, if not stronger than steel. It is made of carbon fibres and it can replace steel in the manufacturing of cars and trucks and in several kinds of building construction which up until now have required steel. The cost of moulding car and truck frames from this material would be cheaper, and the process easier, than using steel. We must always be cautious with the technology which we use.

In several fields what we probably need is what is referred to as intermediate technology. An example for this would be to redevelop the use of water and wind power for turning water wheels to grind rice, pumping water for irrigation, cutting quarry stone, developing electric power, etc. In short, we must develop intermediate technology which is within the reach and skill of common man such as the natural power of water, the wind and the sun.

Because of the tremendous amount of money which the

developed countries have already spent on certain of their industrial sectors, they have been more or less forced to go on doing things the same way they started. Take for example, their continued use of steel and the internal combustion engine in their automobiles. We, as a developing nation, may find it advantageous to skip over this outdated technology and bypass the developed countries.

Once we define for ourselves what economic development is, and once we succeed in achieving the minimal requirements, then we have arrived at the moment when we should consider our future development. Our needs can be identified as 1) sufficiency needs and 2) growth needs.

On this earth there are:

1. Countries which are rich in natural resources and are wealthy, for example the United States and Canada.
2. Countries which are poor in natural resources, but have industry and wealth, for example, Japan.
3. Countries which are rich in natural resources, but poor, for example Third World Countries, including Indonesia.
4. Countries which lack natural resources and are poor, now called Fourth World Countries.

A problem we Indonesians should consider is why countries like Japan, Hong Kong, Singapore and the Netherlands, with poor natural resources, can become rich, while we are rich in natural resources, but remain poor.

In the meantime our world remains one filled with potential danger which can erupt at any time. The need for a new international economic structure remains unresolved. The problem of whites and blacks in South Africa and Rhodesia, the United States' relations with Russia and China, China's relations with Russia, China's future attitude toward Asia, North Vietnam's plans, Indian development, French Canadian separatists' movements, disagreements in Spain and Portugal, the Italian Communist Party's progress, developments among the Arab countries — Syria, Iraq, Egypt, and Saudi Arabia — , contests between Iran and Saudi Arabia, Japan and China, Japan and Russia, and activities of the Russians, the Chinese, the Americans, and the Japanese in Southeast Asia are all factors which could change the world's balance of power. A climatic change which could cause a poor grain harvest in America, Australia, India, Russia, or China could present terrible hardships, for example, for people in various parts of the world.

We need to examine the trade patterns between the countries that produce raw materials and the rich industrial countries. For hundreds of years the wealthy nations have bought materials produced by the efforts of people in poor countries like ours for low prices which they set. They purchased rubber, sugar, coffee, tea, cacao, spices, and natural riches like iron ore, oil, tin, etc. In exchange they sold us things we had very little use for at very high prices. We bought these things because their propaganda and consumer-orientated advertising deceived and entranced us; luxurious cars, TV sets with twelve-channel selections while our country has only one network, and all kinds of other things without which we would have been just as well off and happy.

The people in the United States make up less than 6% of the total number of people on earth and they occupy 6% of the world's land, yet they use almost 50% of the world's resources. In order to maintain the high level of existence in that country each American every year needs:

1,300 pounds of steel

23 pounds of copper

16 pounds of tin

3.5 tons of stone, sand and gravel

500 pounds of cement

400 pounds of soil

200 pounds of salt

100 pounds of phosphate

In aggregate this amounts to 20 tons of material per person which must be taken from the earth.

Suppose that every person in the world, including us, achieved the same standard of living as the Americans. Then the world would need, among other things, the following raw materials:

18 billion tons of iron

300 million tons of copper

200 million tons of zinc

30 million tons of tin

According to statistics produced by world experts this total is more than 100 times the world's current production. The total amount of iron, copper, zinc and tin needed is said to be far in excess of the supply now known to be on earth. This is for our current world population totalling four billion people, and the experts predict that by the year 2000 the population of the world will reach six billion.

Not only are there not enough natural resources for each person to have the luxurious life that has been carried to an extreme in America, but the rich countries will be unable to maintain their standards. In twenty or thirty years they will come to a standstill. Even now their dependence on raw materials from other countries is steadily increasing. The United States now imports approximately 30% of its oil, and Japan more than 90%.

During the years from 1900 to 1961 the import of minerals into the United States increased ten times from $323 million to $3.6 billion. Iron ore, copper, tin, zinc, bauxite, columbium, chromium and cobalt were imported in increasingly large quantities. As far as columbium, chromium and cobalt are concerned, America is now 100% dependent on imports. Only four of the five minerals found in America now are in adequate supply to last her until the year 1984. There are, however, fourteen of them in large enough supply to last after 1984 in the rest of the world. By the year 2000 there will be only three minerals which will remain in sufficient supply in America, and only ten types of minerals in the world, and by 2038 there will be an adequate supply of only eight minerals left on earth. The United States will become a 'have not', and her position will be shared by other industrial countries. France, for example, in 1961 imported 40% of her metals, and around 1985 it is calculated that she will need to import 80%. The Western European economy will be in a similar position. Japan will be in an even more difficult situation because even now almost all the raw materials she requires have to be imported.

One day, not far in the future, the rich societies will have their backs against the wall and they will be faced with the choice of either maintaining their luxurious, extravagant lifestyles by forcing their wishes on the countries which possess the valuable natural resources that they need or changing their life-styles and reverting to a more simple existence. If their attitudes remain the same as they are now, being arrogant with their materialism, wealth and strength, their industry and technology and their political and military power, they will bring various parts of the world to a dangerous level of confrontation. Billions of poor and starving people will face them, and it is not difficult to imagine the resulting disorder and destruction of all things on earth.

There are people in the rich countries who have been thinking for the past five or ten years that they must change the direction and aims of their societies to avoid entering that blind alley and the confrontation between the rich and the poor which would result. The problem is whether changes in consciousness and values in rich societies can occur quickly enough — before we arrive at the final stoplight.

A main characteristic of rich industrialised nations is the large amount of things which people discard, including all types of packaging, starting from cases, paper, plastic, cartons, bottles, porcelain and ceramics and continuing on through machinery, automobiles and other consumer items. In unique American terms this is called 'built-in obsolescence'. Each year automobile and motor companies come out with newer models forcing people who are addicted to the 'new model craze' to buy still newer cars even though the ones they have still function perfectly well. In 1966 alone American statistics indicated that more than $16 billion was spent for packing, wrapping, and storing all kinds of things, and 90% of these materials were later thrown away. Imagine, $16 billion times 415 rupiahs = ?????

We haven't said anything about other kinds of waste in rich societies, nor have we talked about the great powers' multi-billion dollar budgets for the arms race. Although they have SALT I and SALT II, Russia and the United States still compete for military superiority all the time, and each year billions of dollars are spent in the production of all sorts of terrifying weapons.

We have made ourselves followers of the rich consumer-orientated nations. The more we depend on them, be it for capital or technology, the more we rely on their weapons for our safety. This tends to make us further unable to protect our identity as a nation.

If the oil-producing countries are accused of using oil as a tool to blackmail concessions from the rich countries, then we can also accuse the wealthy countries, America for example, of having hundreds of millions of people in a stranglehold due to their dependence on the United States' surplus wheat, rice, corn and other foodstuffs. The food-producing countries now make life or death decisions. The starvation or survival of hundreds of thousands of people is in their hands. If they do not want to sell rice to Indonesia, millions of Indonesians will starve. There is also a dependence on imported food in India, China, even Russia and many other countries. There is no other way open to us. We must free ourselves from dependence on foreign food products. This is the first step we must make. It is our first priority, and we must be thoroughly devoted to it and direct our financial resources and manpower towards achieving it. We must be totally dedicated to this goal.

The number of fish caught in the oceans of the world shows a decline because various areas have been relentlessly over-fished and there is no possibility of restocking them. We know that fish are a basic source of high protein food for human beings. Why haven't we developed the technology to breed fish in the oceans or intertidal zones or bays as we breed cattle on land? There are already people who breed shrimps and oysters!

Facing a world like this, it is very important for us Indonesians to fully develop our capabilities so that we can understand and keep up with the developments and happenings in the world around us now and in the years to come. We need to gather all sorts of information and data concerning world events, not just in science and technology, but also in sociological changes, values and human attitudes.

The developments in communication, data storage and information retrieval systems in the world will surely change man's perceptions in the social, economic, political and artistic fields. This will certainly bring about changes in the relationships of man with man, man with his country, man with nature, man with society and country with country. All this in turn will change man's understanding of power, 'developed economy' and values.

International financial experts are now beginning to worry as they see an increase in money lending throughout the world. They are concerned that a time will come when many borrowing countries will be unable to make interest and debt payments. If just a few countries that owe money were to go bankrupt and be unable to pay their debts, the effect would be tremendous and possibly destroy our entire international monetary system.

The scenario set forth by the international financiers and economists today is this: the key to a healthy world economy lies in the economic well-being of the United States, West Germany and Japan. If a recession in these countries cannot be overcome because, for example, the price of oil is too high, then a world recession could not be stopped and all the world would suffer. The poor countries again would suffer most because of their dependence on foreign aid. Therefore, the raw material producers (including the developing countries) must not demand price increases for their materials. The nations with resources must give the rich countries the chance to maintain their economic growth. This will enable the wealthy nations to buy more products and materials from foreign countries and thus will increase the poor countries' foreign exchange revenues.

There are also experts who say that the rapid economic development rate in rich countries will speed up inflation and this in turn will threaten the international economy. Such experts do not say so, but, in short, the world today is caught up in a vicious circle brought about by the rich countries themselves.

How do we get out of this? We must try hard not to be too dependent on others. We must mobilise our manpower along with our finances. We must be extremely economical, penny pinching if necessary, totally eliminate corruption, and concentrate all our efforts on improving our standard of living. We certainly cannot entirely free ourselves from the international economic system of finance and trade to which we have already opened wide the door of our land. We can, however, continue to make the effort to cushion any possible fall.

If we go on like this, not altering our way of thinking and acting, and not changing the values which guide our lives and our actions, then I am deeply concerned that we will become merely cheap labourers in our own land for the multi-national businesses of Japan, the United States, Germany, Holland, France, England, etc. Are we willing to see our grandchildren experience this fate in their own country?

Now allow me to draw several general conclusions. First, besides the ugly face which we earlier saw in the mirror, there are still many Indonesian characteristics which give us hope. As long as we are completely aware of this we can work at eliminating our bad traits and enhancing our good ones. Second, we must create conditions whereby our people can mature and free themselves from the image of an immature neo-feudal continuation of our feudal past. Third, we see now our need to learn to use the Indonesian language in purer and more precise ways. In short, we should not verbally beat around the bush, but speak our minds. Fourth, we should not continue to turn our backs on ancient Indonesian artistic expressions. They still hold great wealth as a source of inspiration, and they can encourage and develop imaginative spirit and a creative, artistic Indonesian people of today. A statue or piece of copperware from Nias, a drum from Flores or Sumbawa, a Batak or Dayak sculpture, or one from West Irian, woven materials from Lampung, Toraja, Sumbawa, or Timor, a kris from Java, a statue from Mt. Dieng, or an old painting from Bali must at least be considered parallel to the modern works of Affandi, Popo Iskandar, Picasso, or Henry Moore. If you carefully examine Dayak paintings and consider how they see the worlds above and below, you will be struck by their resemblance to the imaginary world of Paul Klee. They seem, as a matter of fact, even more interesting and mysterious.

In this connection we need to build museums which will become living museums where we can associate with the world of our forefathers. We desperately need to watch over our ancient treasures and not allow them to be taken out of our country as they are now.

We need to bring life again to our people's creative arts and crafts. How wonderful it would be if, from elementary school on, children were taught crafts from their respective regions. For example, the schools could give classes in basketry, weaving, batik making, stone and wood carving, etc. Batik and woven materials coming from several areas in our country are twice as lovely as machine-produced textiles. To revitalise our country we must give it colour and design with an Indonesian flavour, and it follows naturally that this will help us find ourselves and our identity in today's world.

I propose that we stop using the word *bapak* for all officials and administrators and that we address each other as *saudara*. Isn't it more pleasant and accurate to say *Saudara* Minister, *Saudara* President, *Saudara* General, *Saudara* Director General, *Saudara* University President? It will not eliminate the close relationship which we wish to maintain.

I propose that we liberate ourselves from feelings of fear and insecurity in expressing what we believe.

I propose that every effort be made to stimulate our culture and arts because these fields will develop our self-respect and enrich our civilisation. Also, through artistic communication we can reach the absolute truth.

I propose a closer involvement of those in private business with the arts. An exchange of ideas would be beneficial to all, tempering strong views with humility.

I propose that we redevelop the power of Indonesians who in ages past sailed to the west as far as Madagascar and Africa and to the east as far as the Polynesian islands. We must re-awaken that Indonesian spirit of ancient times which developed a spice trade through Africa to Rome or across Asia and through the Arabian peninsula to the Mediterranean Sea. We must relive the practices and the bravery of the Buginese sailors who controlled the Indonesian Seas before the arrival of the Portuguese, the Spanish and the Dutch East India Company.

We must redevelop that incentive that once brought us to the peak of our country's artistic success in dance and music, carving and sculpture, architecture like Borobudur and other temples, ornamental art, gold, silver and copper work, weaving and basketry. I am convinced that great artistic talent is still buried within us Indonesians. We must use art and culture as the tools to liberate our country from the shackles of materialism which have long inhibited us and diminished our creativity and inspiration. We must encourage artistic expression in order to re-establish our self-confidence. From ancient times Indonesia has had an affinity with that same culture that spread across the eastern European continent from the Balkans to the Middle East, to the Indian subcontinent and across the Asian continent. This cultural sphere extended throughout the archipelago and the surrounding islands.

I propose, ah........what do I wish to propose? I propose that we Indonesians, act in a more humanitarian way toward other creatures in the world.

I propose that we strive to understand ourselves better and to handle our country's problems by ourselves, think for ourselves and be capable of doing things for ourselves.

I propose that we reassert our ethical values, that we develop a sensitivity that will enable us to differentiate between right and wrong, between the appropriate and the inappropriate, between self-interest and the best interests of our society and between what is just and what is despotic. We must not apply this ethical code only to ourselves and our equals, but to all humanity, to all who suffer, are oppressed and live in infinite misery on the face of this earth.

I propose that we extend this attitude to include God's other creatures and creations — all wild animals and plants, mountains, forests, water, air, land, and our islands, which we must guard and protect from destruction.

This is my blueprint to be used for extending solidarity to the unborn Indonesian generations in order that they may also enjoy our land, which is still green and fertile and full of all kinds of fascinating and beautiful life, and that they may also continue to exist.

Also, it is now vitally important to develop an educational system which can meet the challenges of today's world. Every year in every field of science and technology tens of thousands of reports and articles are published in dozens of languages. In America, for example, the number of publications is tremendous, as also in Japan, Russia, France and Germany. All their scholars and other interested people are unable to keep up with this amount of printed matter so a special service is needed to summarise the information. Even with such a service there is still too much data to handle, and more sorting and condensing is necessary to give a clear picture of current developments in each field.

There are vast amounts of information which we must continuously pursue, gather and absorb, and for this we need knowledgeable people who are understanding, sympathetic, honest and dedicated.

In closing I offer a Minangkabau proverb:

Tambilang di bawah langsek	I have told you all I know;
Tasisik di bawah lantai	The rest, that I know not,
Dibilang sado nan dapek	I must leave to others —
Nan tingga untuk nan pandai	To those who know more than I.

And also a word of advice, the essence of high Javanese philosophy:

> *Sing ana, ora ana, sing ora ana, ana.*
>
> What you are after is not available,
> What you are not after is everywhere.